Math Expressions

Homework and Remembering • Volume 2

Developed by
The Children's Math Worlds Research Project

PROJECT DIRECTOR AND AUTHOR
Dr. Karen C. Fuson

This material is based upon work supported by the
National Science Foundation
under Grant Numbers
ESI-9816320, REC-9806020, and RED-935373.

Any opinions, findings, and conclusions, or recommendations expressed in this material
are those of the author and do not necessarily reflect the views of the National Science Foundation.

HOUGHTON MIFFLIN HARCOURT

Teacher Reviewers

Kindergarten
Patricia Stroh Sugiyama
Wilmette, Illinois

Barbara Wahle
Evanston, Illinois

Grade 1
Sandra Budson
Newton, Massachusetts

Janet Pecci
Chicago, Illinois

Megan Rees
Chicago, Illinois

Grade 2
Molly Dunn
Danvers, Massachusetts

Agnes Lesnick
Hillside, Illinois

Rita Soto
Chicago, Illinois

Grade 3
Jane Curran
Honesdale, Pennsylvania

Sandra Tucker
Chicago, Illinois

Grade 4
Sara Stoneberg Llibre
Chicago, Illinois

Sheri Roedel
Chicago, Illinois

Grade 5
Todd Atler
Chicago, Illinois

Leah Barry
Norfolk, Massachusetts

Special Thanks

Special thanks to the many teachers, students, parents, principals, writers, researchers, and work-study students who participated in the Children's Math Worlds Research Project over the years.

Credits

(t) © G. K. Hart/Vikki Hart/Getty Images, (b) Photodisc/Getty Images.

Illustrative art: Ginna Magee and Burgandy Beam/Wilkinson Studio; Tim Johnson
Technical art: Anthology, Inc.

Name _____

Homework

Fill in the partners to complete the partner equation.

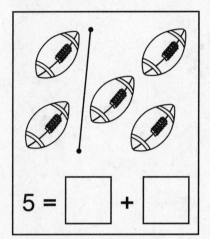

5 = ☐ + ☐

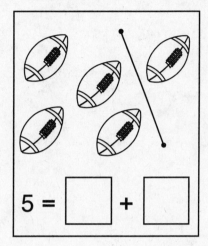

5 = ☐ + ☐

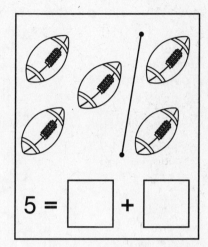

5 = ☐ + ☐

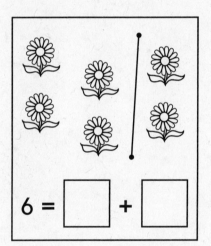

6 = ☐ + ☐

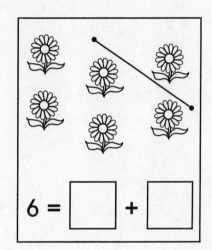

6 = ☐ + ☐

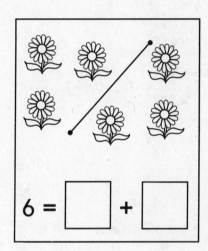

6 = ☐ + ☐

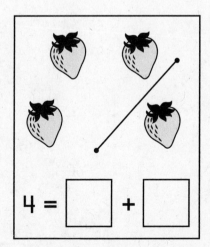

4 = ☐ + ☐

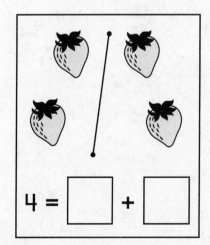

4 = ☐ + ☐

➡ **On the Back** Draw a picture with shapes.

Name

Find Partners of 10

Practice

Draw a line to show the partners. Write the partners.

10 = ☐ + ☐

10 = ☐ + ☐

10 = ☐ + ☐

10 = ☐ + ☐

10 = ☐ + ☐

10 = ☐ + ☐

10 = ☐ + ☐

10 = ☐ + ☐

10 = ☐ + ☐

On the Back Draw your own patterns.

Name

Teen Numbers and Equations

Homework

Name _____

Continue the pattern.

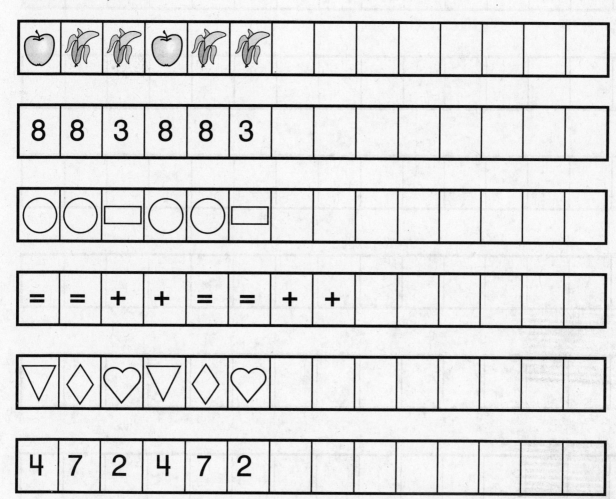

Draw your own patterns.

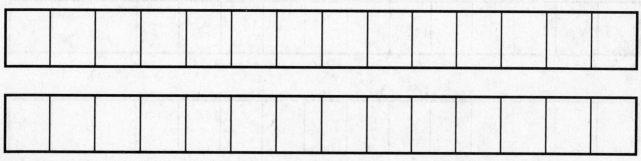

🡆 **On the Back** Draw your own patterns.

Name

Addition and Subtraction Stories: Grocery Store Scenario

4–6

Homework

Name _____

Write the partners.

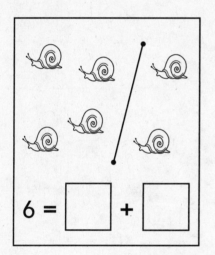

5 = ☐ + ☐

5 = ☐ + ☐

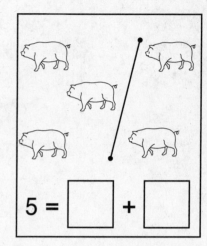

5 = ☐ + ☐

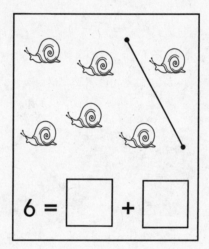

6 = ☐ + ☐

6 = ☐ + ☐

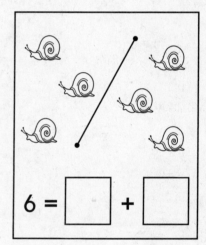

6 = ☐ + ☐

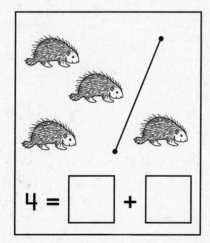

4 = ☐ + ☐

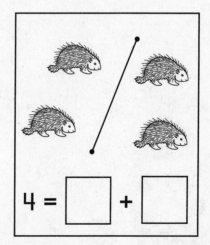

4 = ☐ + ☐

On the Back Draw a picture for the equation 6 = 2 + 4. Draw the Break-Apart Stick.

UNIT 4 LESSON 6

Patterns with Shapes and Repeating Patterns **105**

Copyright © Houghton Mifflin Company. All rights reserved.

Patterns with Shapes and Repeating Patterns

Homework

Write the partners.

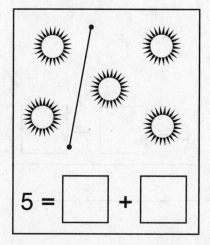

5 = ☐ + ☐

5 = ☐ + ☐

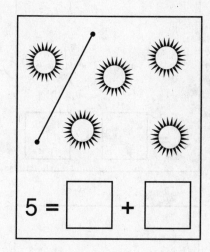

5 = ☐ + ☐

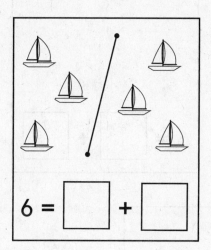

6 = ☐ + ☐

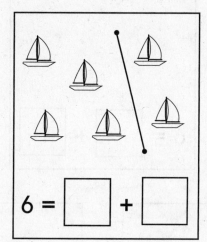

6 = ☐ + ☐

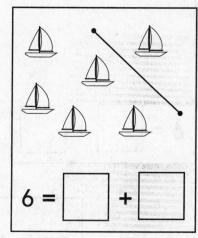

6 = ☐ + ☐

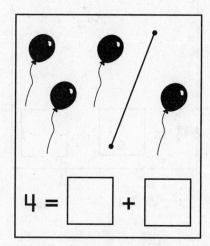

4 = ☐ + ☐

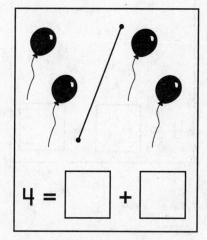

4 = ☐ + ☐

🡆 **On the Back** Make your own partner drawings. Write the partners.

5 = ☐ + ☐

5 = ☐ + ☐

5 = ☐ + ☐

6 = ☐ + ☐

6 = ☐ + ☐

6 = ☐ + ☐

4 = ☐ + ☐

4 = ☐ + ☐

More Teen Numbers and Equations

Name _____

Practice

Count and write how many. Ring fewer.

3	(**2**)	☐	☐
☐	☐	☐	☐
☐	☐	☐	☐
☐	☐	☐	☐

Write the numbers 1 through 20.

➡ **On the Back** Make your own partner drawings. Write the partners.

More Patterns with Shapes **109**

5 = [ ] + [ ]

5 = [ ] + [ ]

5 = [ ] + [ ]

6 = [ ] + [ ]

6 = [ ] + [ ]

6 = [ ] + [ ]

4 = [ ] + [ ]

4 = [ ] + [ ]

Homework

Draw a line to show the partners. Write the partners.

6 = ☐ + ☐

10 = ☐ + ☐

6 = ☐ + ☐

10 = ☐ + ☐

6 = ☐ + ☐

10 = ☐ + ☐

5 = ☐ + ☐

10 = ☐ + ☐

10 = ☐ + ☐

5 = ☐ + ☐

4 = ☐ + ☐   4 = ☐ + ☐

 On the Back Make your own partner drawings. Write the partners.

5 = ☐ + ☐

5 = ☐ + ☐

6 = ☐ + ☐

6 = ☐ + ☐

6 = ☐ + ☐

6 = ☐ + ☐

4 = ☐ + ☐

4 = ☐ + ☐

Practice

Count and write how many. Ring more.

4 (ringed)	3	☐	☐	☐	☐
☐	☐	☐	☐	☐	☐
☐	☐	☐	☐	☐	☐
☐	☐	☐	☐	☐	☐

Write the numbers from 1 through 20.

➡ **On the Back** Write the numbers 1–30, then 11–30, and then 1–50.

Numbers Through 30

Name _____

Homework

Count and write how many. Ring more.

⭕ **4** ☐ **1**	☐ ☐	☐ ☐
☐ ☐	☐ ☐	☐ ☐
☐ ☐	☐ ☐	☐ ☐
☐ ☐	☐ ☐	☐ ☐

Write the numbers 11 through 30.

11								

➡ **On the Back** Write the numbers 1–30, then 11–30, and then 1–50.

Addition and Subtraction Drawings: Grocery Store Scenario **115**

Addition and Subtraction Drawings: Grocery Store Scenario

Name _____

Practice

Count and write how many. Draw lines to match. Ring the extra things.
Write M for more and F for fewer.

| 7 | M |

| 6 | F |

| ☐ | ___ |

| ☐ | ___ |

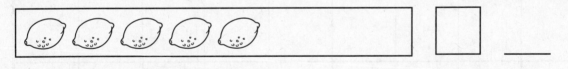

| ☐ | ___ |

| ☐ | ___ |

| ☐ | ___ |

| ☐ | ___ |

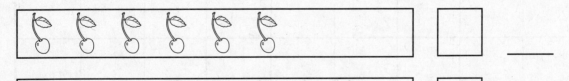

| ☐ | ___ |

| ☐ | ___ |

On the Back Write the numbers 1–30, then 11–30, and then 1–50.

Name _____

More Patterns with Shapes and Repeating Patterns

Name _____

Homework

Draw Tiny Tumblers on the Math Mountains.

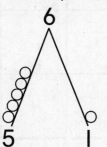
6
5   1

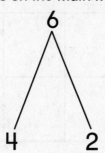
6
4   2

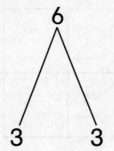
6
3   3

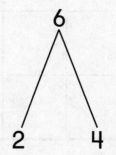
6
2   4

6
1   5

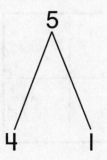
5
4   1

5
3   2

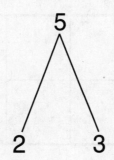
5
2   3

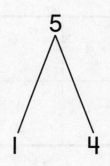
5
1   4

2
1   1

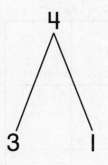
4
3   1

4
2   2

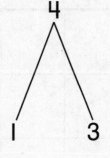
4
1   3

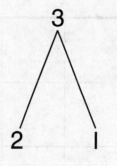
3
2   1

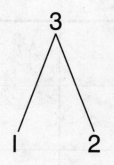
3
1   2

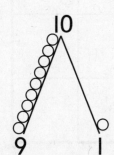
10
9   1

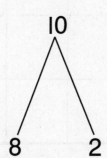
10
8   2

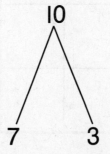
10
7   3

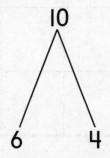
10
6   4

10
5   5

 On the Back Write the numbers 1–30, then 11–30, and then 1–50.

Partners of 10 with 5-Groups

Homework

Draw Tiny Tumblers on the Math Mountains.

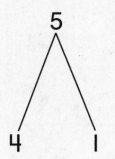
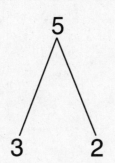
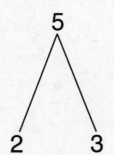
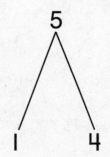
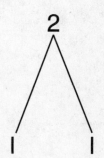

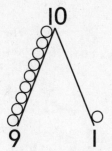
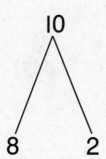
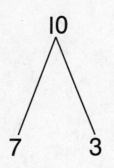

Write the numbers 1 through 40.

➡ **On the Back** Make a picture with shapes.

Name _____

Homework

1. Draw lines to match.

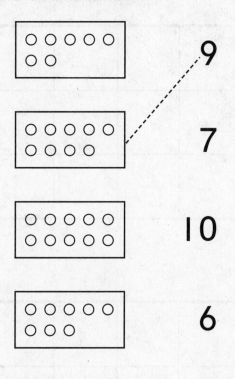

9

7

10

6

8

2. Make two matches.

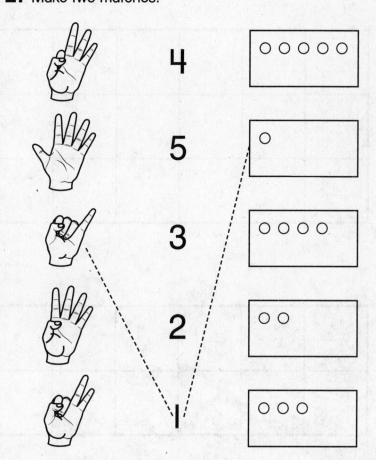

4

5

3

2

1

3. Connect the dots in order.

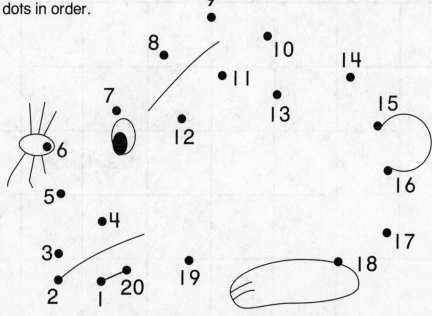

🡢 **On the Back** Write the numbers 1–30, then 11–30, and then 1–50.

2- and 3-Dimensional Shapes: Triangles **123**

Name

2- and 3-Dimensional Shapes: Triangles

Name _____

Practice

Draw Tiny Tumblers on the Math Mountains.

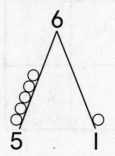 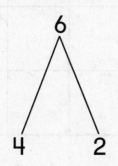 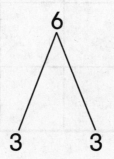 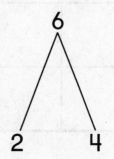 

   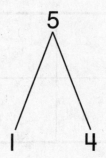 

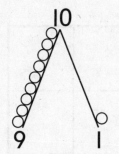    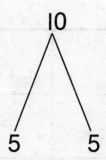

Write the numbers 11 through 30.

 On the Back Write the numbers 1–30, then 11–30, and then 1–50.

Vertical Graphs and Comparisons **125**

Name _____

(blank grid — 10 columns × 3 rows)

(blank grid — 10 columns × 2 rows)

(blank grid — 10 columns × 5 rows)

Vertical Graphs and Comparisons

Name _____

Homework

Continue the pattern.

| p | b | b | p | b | b | | | | | | | | |

| E | E | 3 | E | E | 3 | | | | | | | | |

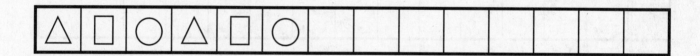

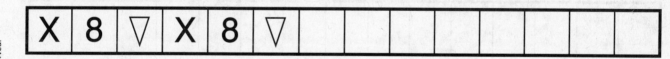

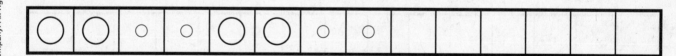

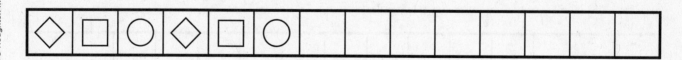

🡲 **On the Back** Draw your own patterns.

Equations: Partners of 3, 4, 5, 6, and 10 **127**

Equations: Partners of 3, 4, 5, 6, and 10

Name _____

Practice

Draw a line to show the partners. Write the partners.

6 = ☐ + ☐

6 = ☐ + ☐

6 = ☐ + ☐

5 = ☐ + ☐

5 = ☐ + ☐

10 = ☐ + ☐

10 = ☐ + ☐

10 = ☐ + ☐

10 = ☐ + ☐

10 = ☐ + ☐

10 = ☐ + ☐

4 = ☐ + ☐   4 = ☐ + ☐

➡ **On the Back** Add the numbers.

Triangles and Addition and Subtraction Stories **129**

1 + 4 = ☐

4 + 1 = ☐

1 + 3 = ☐

1 + 2 = ☐

2 + 3 = ☐

1 + 5 = ☐

3 + 4 = ☐

4 + 3 = ☐

2 + 7 = ☐

1 + 1 = ☐

2 + 3 = ☐

3 + 0 = ☐

2 + 2 = ☐

3 + 2 = ☐

1 + 8 = ☐

9 + 1 = ☐

5 + 1 = ☐

6 + 3 = ☐

1 + 2 = ☐

3 + 1 = ☐

2 + 1 = ☐

1 + 3 = ☐

5 + 0 = ☐

3 + 7 = ☐

4 + 4 = ☐

5 + 5 = ☐

3 + 5 = ☐

Triangles and Addition and Subtraction Stories

Homework

Add the numbers.

2 + 2 = ☐   0 + 2 = ☐   1 + 2 = ☐

3 + 1 = ☐   1 + 4 = ☐   5 + 0 = ☐

4 + 0 = ☐   2 + 3 = ☐   1 + 3 = ☐

2 + 1 = ☐   0 + 5 = ☐   1 + 1 = ☐

3 + 2 = ☐   4 + 1 = ☐   2 + 3 = ☐

Connect the dots in order.

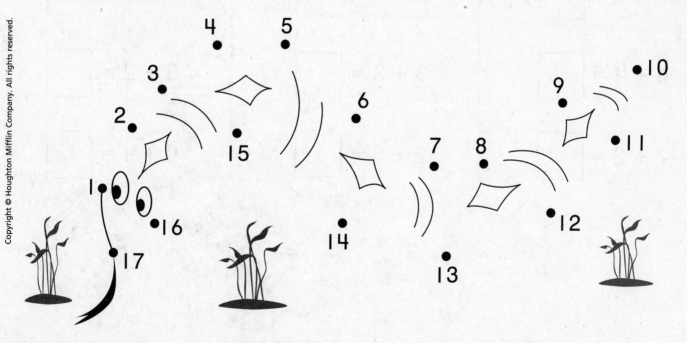

⬤ **On the Back** Add the numbers.

Horizontal Graphs and Comparisons **131**

3 + 0 = ☐

2 + 2 = ☐

1 + 4 = ☐

2 + 3 = ☐

0 + 4 = ☐

4 + 5 = ☐

1 + 9 = ☐

6 + 4 = ☐

7 + 2 = ☐

1 + 3 = ☐

2 + 1 = ☐

1 + 3 = ☐

3 + 2 = ☐

3 + 1 = ☐

6 + 3 = ☐

3 + 6 = ☐

3 + 3 = ☐

2 + 5 = ☐

3 + 2 = ☐

4 + 1 = ☐

1 + 2 = ☐

4 + 1 = ☐

1 + 1 = ☐

4 + 3 = ☐

2 + 4 = ☐

5 + 2 = ☐

4 + 4 = ☐

Horizontal Graphs and Comparisons

Homework

Write each number and circle which is fewer.

3	(1)	☐ ☐	☐ ☐
☐	☐	☐	☐
☐	☐	☐	☐
☐	☐	☐	☐

Write the numbers 11 through 30.

→ **On the Back** Add the numbers.

Shapes in a Butterfly Scene **133**

2 + 3 = ☐   1 + 4 = ☐   1 + 3 = ☐

3 + 2 = ☐   1 + 2 = ☐   3 + 1 = ☐

0 + 4 = ☐   1 + 1 = ☐   2 + 2 = ☐

2 + 3 = ☐   5 + 0 = ☐   4 + 1 = ☐

4 + 1 = ☐   2 + 1 = ☐   1 + 2 = ☐

5 + 2 = ☐   3 + 6 = ☐   5 + 4 = ☐

6 + 1 = ☐   8 + 2 = ☐   1 + 5 = ☐

4 + 4 = ☐   7 + 1 = ☐   3 + 3 = ☐

4 + 5 = ☐   2 + 4 = ☐   7 + 3 = ☐

Shapes in a Butterfly Scene

Homework

Name _____

Continue the pattern.

| Z | N | N | Z | N | N | | | | | | | | |

| ▽ | △ | △ | △ | ▽ | △ | △ | △ | | | | | | |

| 7 | 7 | 8 | 8 | 7 | 7 | 8 | 8 | | | | | | |

| ◯ | ◯ | ◯ | • | ◯ | ◯ | ◯ | • | | | | | | |

| R | K | L | R | K | L | R | K | L | | | | | |

| | | ♡ | — | | | ♡ | — | | | ♡ | — | | | | | |

| 3 | 7 | 9 | 3 | 7 | 9 | 3 | 7 | 9 | | | | | |

| C | C | C | D | C | C | C | D | | | | | | |

| ▢ | ◯ | ◯ | ◯ | ▢ | ◯ | ◯ | ◯ | | | | | | |

⬤ **On the Back** Draw your own patterns.

Partners of 10: Stars in the Night Sky **135**

Name _____

Partners of 10: Stars in the Night Sky

Homework

Name _____

Ring the 10-group in the picture. Write the equation with tens and ones.

__10__ + __9__ = __19__

_____ + _____ = _____

_____ + _____ = _____

_____ + _____ = _____

_____ + _____ = _____

_____ + _____ = _____

_____ + _____ = _____

_____ + _____ = _____

 On the Back Choose a teen number. Draw that number of circles. Make a 10-group.

Solve and Retell Story Problems **137**

Name

Solve and Retell Story Problems

Name _____

Practice

Subtract the numbers. Use your fingers or draw.

4 + 1 = ☐   3 + 3 = ☐   5 + 4 = ☐

3 + 2 = ☐   5 + 3 = ☐   2 + 2 = ☐

2 + 0 = ☐   4 + 2 = ☐   4 + 3 = ☐

5 + 2 = ☐   3 + 1 = ☐   5 + 1 = ☐

2 + 1 = ☐   4 + 0 = ☐   4 + 2 = ☐

Equal or unequal? = or ≠	Equal or unequal? = or ≠	Equal or unequal? = or ≠
3 2 + 1	● ●	1 0 + 2
2 2 + 2	○ ○ ○	3 1 + 2
1 3 + 2	● ●	2 2 + 3
4 1 + 3	○ ○ ○	5 4 + 1
5 3 + 0	●	4 1 + 2

➡ **On the Back** Write the numbers 1–100.

Name

1	2								10
11									
									100

Make Quantities 1–20

Homework

Think 5-groups to solve quickly. Then color each balloon.

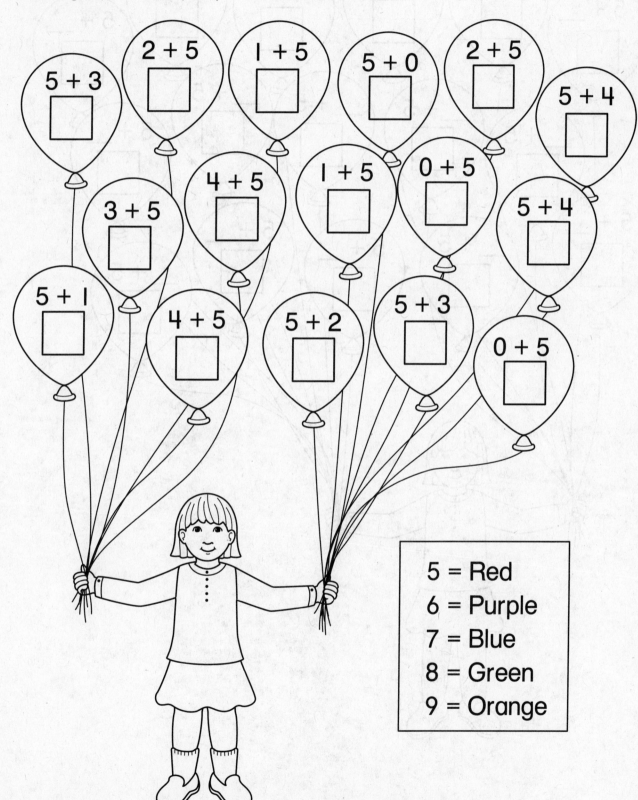

5 + 3

2 + 5

1 + 5

5 + 0

2 + 5

5 + 4

3 + 5

4 + 5

1 + 5

0 + 5

5 + 4

5 + 1

4 + 5

5 + 2

5 + 3

0 + 5

5 = Red
6 = Purple
7 = Blue
8 = Green
9 = Orange

On the Back Make and answer your own 5-group problems.

Geometric Patterns and Rotations   **141**

Geometric Patterns and Rotations

Homework

Ring the 10-group. Write the ten and ones in each equation.

$$\underline{\quad 10 \quad} + \underline{\quad 3 \quad} = \underline{\quad 13 \quad}$$ $$\underline{\quad\quad} + \underline{\quad\quad} = \underline{\quad\quad}$$

$$\underline{\quad\quad} + \underline{\quad\quad} = \underline{\quad\quad}$$ $$\underline{\quad\quad} + \underline{\quad\quad} = \underline{\quad\quad}$$

$$\underline{\quad\quad} + \underline{\quad\quad} = \underline{\quad\quad}$$ $$\underline{\quad\quad} + \underline{\quad\quad} = \underline{\quad\quad}$$

$$\underline{\quad\quad} + \underline{\quad\quad} = \underline{\quad\quad}$$ $$\underline{\quad\quad} + \underline{\quad\quad} = \underline{\quad\quad}$$

$$\underline{\quad\quad} + \underline{\quad\quad} = \underline{\quad\quad}$$ $$\underline{\quad\quad} + \underline{\quad\quad} = \underline{\quad\quad}$$

⬤ **On the Back** Make a picture with shapes.

Patterns in Numbers 1–20

Name _____

Practice

Continue the pattern.

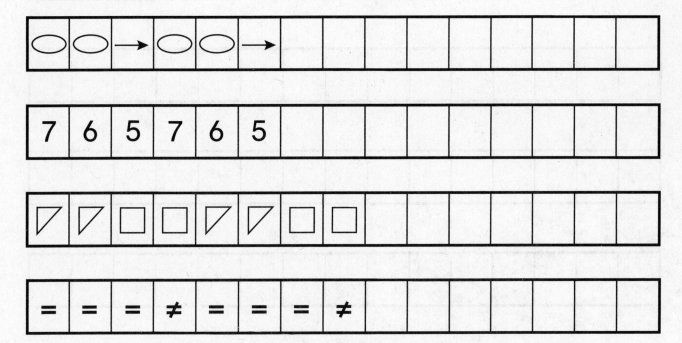

A B B B A B B B ▢ ▢ ▢ ▢ ▢ ▢ ▢ ▢ ▢ ▢ ▢ ▢

V W X V W X ▢ ▢ ▢ ▢ ▢ ▢ ▢ ▢ ▢ ▢ ▢ ▢ ▢ ▢

Draw your own patterns.

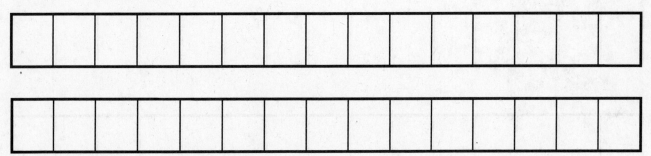

⟹ **On the Back** Draw your own patterns.

Name _____

Review Partners of 2, 3, 4, 5, 6, and 10

Draw circles to show each number.
Write the ten and the ones under the circles.

11	12	13	14 15	16	17	18	19 20

10 + 1   10 +   +   +   +   +   +   +

Complete the equations. Discuss patterns you see.

12 = 10 + ___   14 = 10 + ___   19 = 10 + ___   15 = 10 + ___

16 = 10 + ___   17 = 10 + ___   18 = 10 + ___   13 = 10 + ___

On the Back Add the numbers.

Name _____

1 + 0 = ☐   2 + 1 = ☐   2 + 3 = ☐

3 + 1 = ☐   2 + 2 = ☐   1 + 1 = ☐

4 + 1 = ☐   1 + 2 = ☐   3 + 2 = ☐

3 + 1 = ☐   1 + 4 = ☐   4 + 1 = ☐

1 + 3 = ☐   4 + 0 = ☐   1 + 2 = ☐

4 + 5 = ☐   3 + 4 = ☐   2 + 8 = ☐

1 + 7 = ☐   3 + 7 = ☐   4 + 4 = ☐

9 + 1 = ☐   8 + 2 = ☐   2 + 7 = ☐

1 + 5 = ☐   5 + 4 = ☐   4 + 2 = ☐

Name _____

Practice

Draw Tiny Tumblers on the Math Mountains. Write the partners.

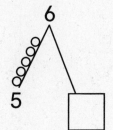 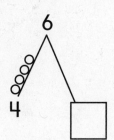 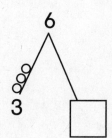 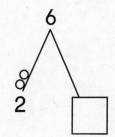 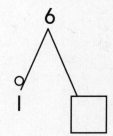

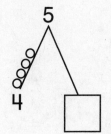 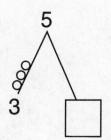 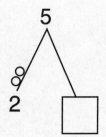 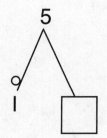 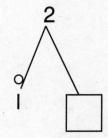

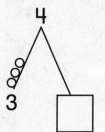 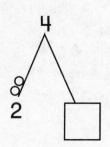 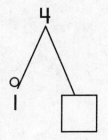 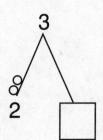 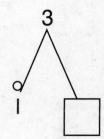

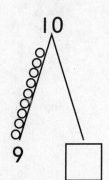 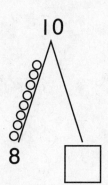 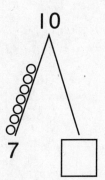 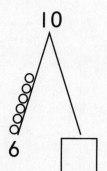 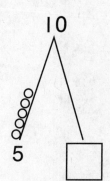

On the Back Draw four different Math Mountains for 9.

Tens in Teen Numbers: A Game

Homework

Think 5-groups to find the totals. Then color each balloon.

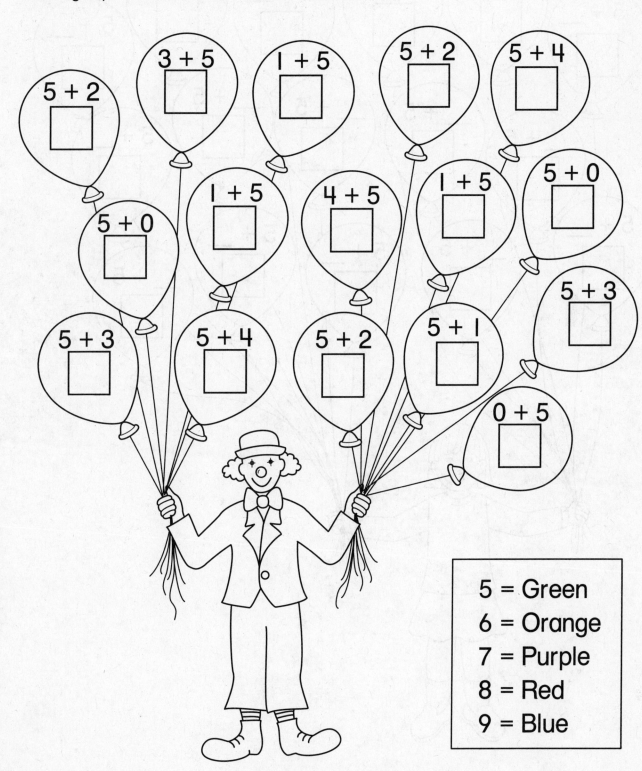

5 = Green
6 = Orange
7 = Purple
8 = Red
9 = Blue

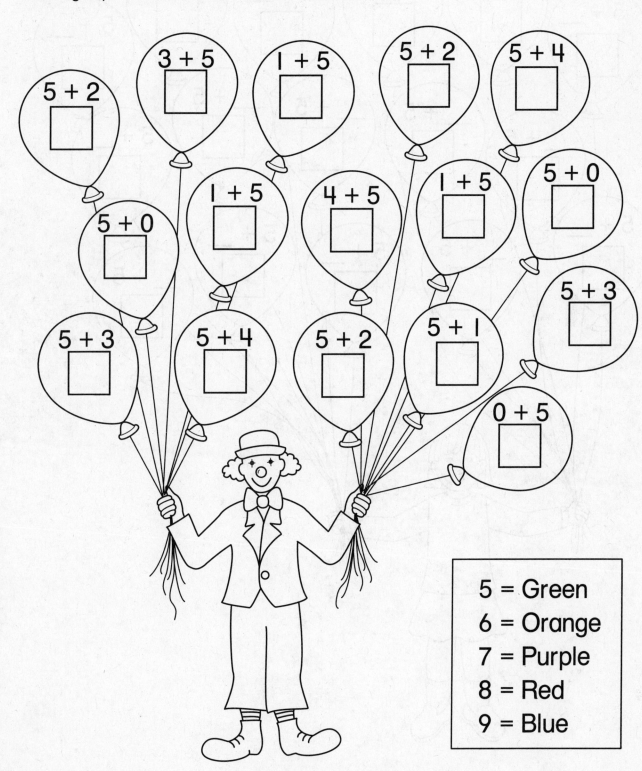 **On the Back** Make and answer your own 5-group problems.

5 + ___ ☐

___ + 5 ☐

___ + 5 ☐

5 + ___ ☐

___ + 5 ☐

5 + ___ ☐

___ + 5 ☐

___ + 5 ☐

___ + 5 ☐

___ + 5 ☐

5 + ___ ☐

5 + ___ ☐

___ + 5 ☐

5 + ___ ☐

5 + ___ ☐

___ + 5 ☐

Tens in Teen Numbers Book

Name _____

Practice

Subtract the numbers. Use your fingers or draw.

5 − 1 = ☐   5 − 3 = ☐   4 − 0 = ☐

5 − 2 = ☐   5 − 4 = ☐   2 − 1 = ☐

5 − 0 = ☐   4 − 3 = ☐   4 − 1 = ☐

4 − 2 = ☐   3 − 2 = ☐   5 − 1 = ☐

3 − 1 = ☐   3 − 0 = ☐   5 − 2 = ☐

Equal or unequal?   Equal or unequal?   Equal or unequal?
    = or ≠   = or ≠   = or ≠

2   0 + 1   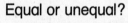   5   1 + 4

1   3 + 1      3   2 + 3

3   2 + 1      4   3 + 2

5   2 + 3   1   2 + 1

4   3 + 0   2   0 + 2

 On the Back Write the numbers 1–100.

1	11								
2									
10									100

Partners of 10: Class Project

Name _____

Homework

Subtract the numbers. Use your fingers or draw.

4 − 1 = ☐   5 − 1 = ☐   4 − 2 = ☐

2 − 2 = ☐   4 − 0 = ☐   5 − 0 = ☐

3 − 0 = ☐   5 − 3 = ☐   4 − 3 = ☐

5 − 2 = ☐   3 − 2 = ☐   2 − 1 = ☐

3 − 1 = ☐   1 − 0 = ☐   5 − 5 = ☐

Equal or unequal? = or ≠		Equal or unequal? = or ≠	Equal or unequal? = or ≠
		10 2 + 7	8 5 + 3
		6 4 + 2	6 4 + 3
		9 4 + 4	9 2 + 5
		7 2 + 6	7 1 + 6
		8 4 + 3	5 3 + 3

➡ **On the Back** Write the numbers 1–120.

Introduction to Counting and Grouping Routines **155**

1	2								10
11									
21									
									100
									120

Introduction to Counting and Grouping Routines

Homework

Name _____

Draw Tiny Tumblers and write how many are on each Math Mountain.

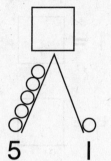 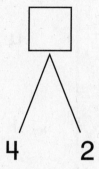 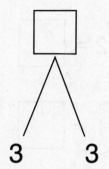 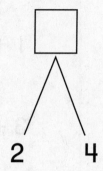 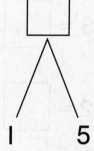

5 1 4 2 3 3 2 4 1 5

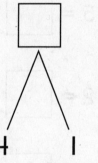 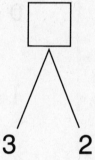 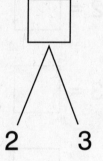 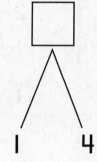 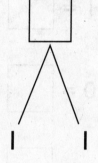

4 1 3 2 2 3 1 4 1 1

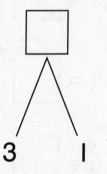 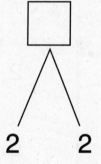 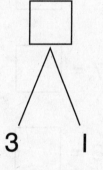 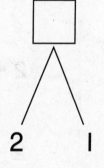 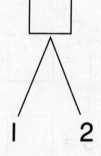

3 1 2 2 3 1 2 1 1 2

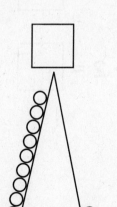  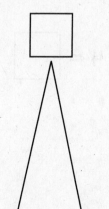 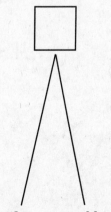 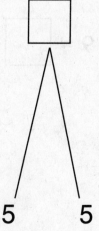

9 1 8 2 7 3 6 4 5 5

➡ **On the Back** Add the numbers.

Add Partners to Find Totals **157**

3 + 1 = ☐

2 + 3 = ☐

3 + 2 = ☐

1 + 1 = ☐

3 + 0 = ☐

2 + 4 = ☐

7 + 1 = ☐

4 + 3 = ☐

1 + 9 = ☐

1 + 4 = ☐

1 + 2 = ☐

3 + 1 = ☐

2 + 2 = ☐

1 + 3 = ☐

8 + 1 = ☐

2 + 7 = ☐

2 + 8 = ☐

4 + 4 = ☐

2 + 1 = ☐

4 + 1 = ☐

1 + 4 = ☐

0 + 5 = ☐

1 + 2 = ☐

5 + 3 = ☐

2 + 4 = ☐

4 + 5 = ☐

6 + 2 = ☐

Add Partners to Find Totals

Practice

Draw Tiny Tumblers and write how many are on each Math Mountain.

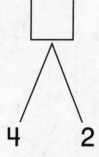 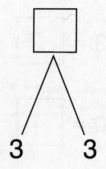 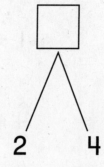 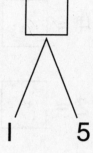
5   1   4   2   3   3   2   4   1   5

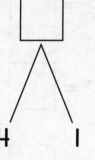 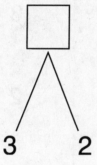 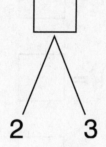 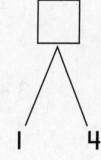 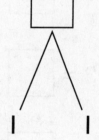
4   1   3   2   2   3   1   4   1   1

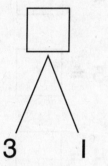 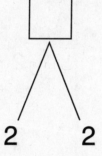 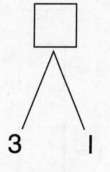 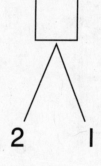 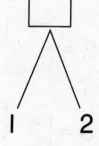
3   1   2   2   3   1   2   1   1   2

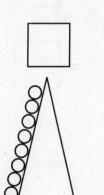  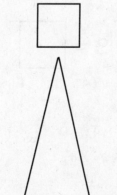  
9   1   8   2   7   3   6   4   5   5

On the Back Add the numbers.

1 + 3 = ☐

1 + 4 = ☐

3 + 2 = ☐

2 + 1 = ☐

2 + 3 = ☐

3 + 5 = ☐

5 + 2 = ☐

3 + 3 = ☐

4 + 2 = ☐

2 + 1 = ☐

1 + 3 = ☐

4 + 0 = ☐

1 + 1 = ☐

3 + 1 = ☐

4 + 3 = ☐

7 + 3 = ☐

8 + 1 = ☐

6 + 3 = ☐

4 + 1 = ☐

0 + 3 = ☐

1 + 2 = ☐

3 + 2 = ☐

2 + 2 = ☐

8 + 2 = ☐

2 + 5 = ☐

4 + 4 = ☐

1 + 7 = ☐

Story Problems: Totals Under 10

Homework

3 - 2 = ☐

2 - 1 = ☐

5 - 1 = ☐

4 - 4 = ☐

10 - 1 = ☐

6 - 4 = ☐

7 - 3 = ☐

10 - 4 = ☐

7 - 3 = ☐

5 - 2 = ☐

3 - 1 = ☐

8 - 1 = ☐

9 - 3 = ☐

5 - 3 = ☐

7 - 2 = ☐

9 - 4 = ☐

6 - 1 = ☐

6 - 5 = ☐

8 - 4 = ☐

6 - 2 = ☐

4 - 0 = ☐

9 - 1 = ☐

4 - 2 = ☐

2 - 2 = ☐

6 - 1 = ☐

10 - 2 = ☐

8 - 2 = ☐

On the Back Make a picture that shows two equal group of shapes.

Subtract to Make Equal Groups

Name _____

Homework

Continue the pattern.

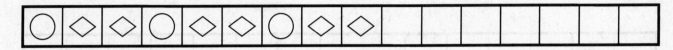

| 3 | 9 | 9 | 9 | 3 | 9 | 9 | 9 | | | | | | | | |

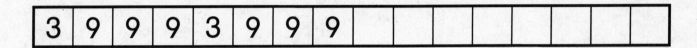

| | | | | | | | | | | | | | | | |

| 2 | 2 | 8 | 2 | 2 | 8 | 2 | 2 | 8 | | | | | | | |

| 4 | 6 | 7 | 4 | 6 | 7 | 4 | 6 | 7 | | | | | | | |

| J | J | J | K | J | J | J | K | | | | | | | | |

| P | R | R | R | P | R | R | R | | | | | | | | |

→ **On the Back** Draw your own patterns.

Practice: Pattern Block and Attribute Card Activities **163**

Name _____

Practice: Pattern Block and Attribute Card Activities

Name _____

Homework

Circle the ten. Write the ten and ones in each equation.

___10___ + ___8___ = ___18___

_____ + _____ = _____

_____ + _____ = _____

_____ + _____ = _____

_____ + _____ = _____

_____ + _____ = _____

_____ + _____ = _____

_____ + _____ = _____

_____ + _____ = _____

_____ + _____ = _____

 **On the Back** Subtract the numbers.

More Horizontal Graphs and Comparisons **165**

5 − 3 = ☐   4 − 1 = ☐   5 − 5 = ☐

4 − 0 = ☐   5 − 1 = ☐   3 − 2 = ☐

1 − 1 = ☐   3 − 1 = ☐   5 − 4 = ☐

4 − 3 = ☐   5 − 0 = ☐   3 − 3 = ☐

5 − 2 = ☐   2 − 1 = ☐   4 − 2 = ☐

7 − 5 = ☐   8 − 3 = ☐   10 − 2 = ☐

6 − 5 = ☐   10 − 3 = ☐   8 − 2 = ☐

9 − 4 = ☐   8 − 1 = ☐   8 − 5 = ☐

6 − 2 = ☐   9 − 5 = ☐   7 − 4 = ☐

Name _____

Homework

Ring the shape that shows halves.

1.

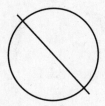 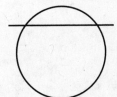

2.

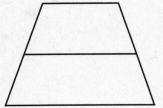 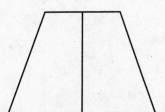

Use pennies.

Then draw what you did.

3. Use 10 pennies. Make 2 groups.

 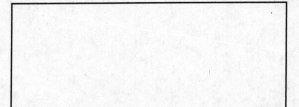

4. Use 8 pennies. Make 4 groups.

⬅ **On the Back** Use 12 pennies. Make 2 equal groups.

Equal Parts, Equal Shares **167**

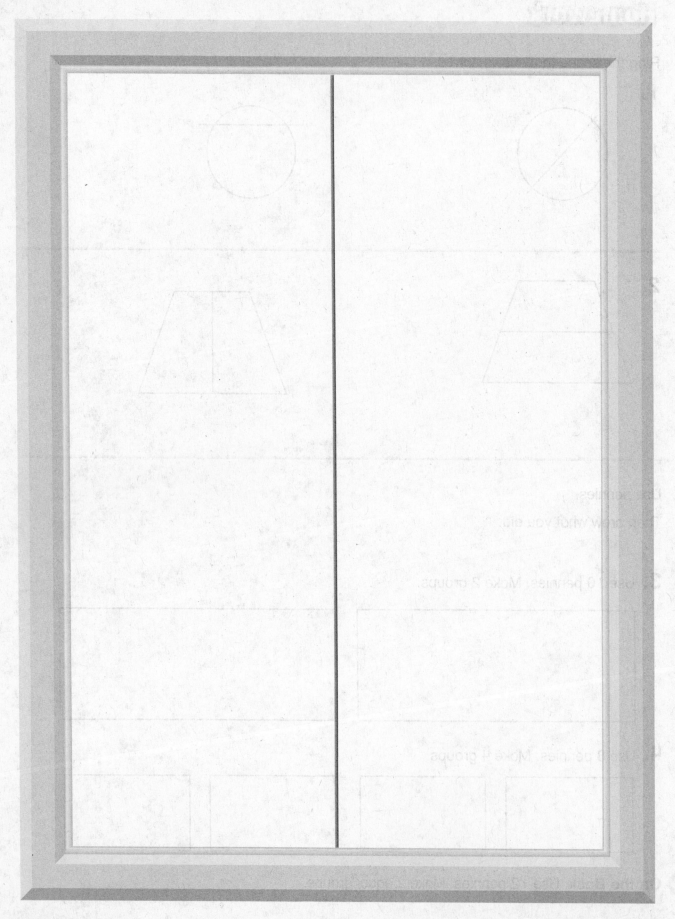

Equal Parts, Equal Shares

Think of 5-groups to help you solve. Then color each balloon.

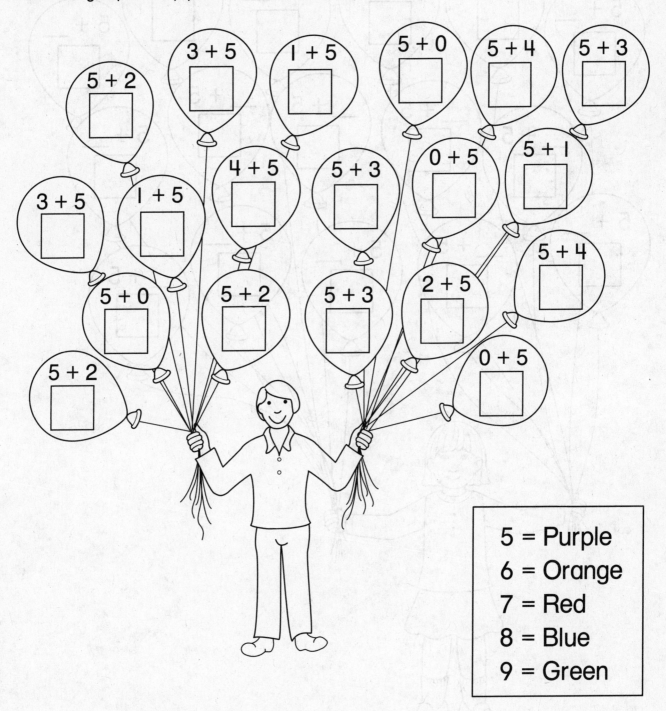

5 + 2

3 + 5

1 + 5

5 + 0

5 + 4

5 + 3

3 + 5

1 + 5

4 + 5

5 + 3

0 + 5

5 + 1

5 + 0

5 + 2

5 + 3

2 + 5

5 + 4

5 + 2

0 + 5

5 = Purple
6 = Orange
7 = Red
8 = Blue
9 = Green

On the Back Make and answer your own 5-group problems.

Shapes in a Robot Scene

Homework

Ring **True** or **Not True**.

Draw a picture to show why.

Rectangles have 5 corners.   True   Not True

5 and 2 are partners of 7.   True   Not True

8 squares are more than 6 squares.   True   Not True

5 and 1 are partners of 4.   True   Not True

 On the Back Draw a rectangle. Count the corners.

Name

Use Mathematical Processes

Homework

Write the letter.

Write the value of each coin.

| Penny = P | Nickel = N | Dime = D |

  P   I¢

 _____ _____

 _____ _____

 _____ _____

 _____ _____

 _____ _____

 _____ _____

 _____ _____

 _____ _____

 _____ _____

 _____ _____

 _____ _____

 _____ _____

 _____ _____

 On the Back Subtract the numbers.

$5 - 2 = \boxed{}$

$4 - 1 = \boxed{}$

$5 - 5 = \boxed{}$

$2 - 0 = \boxed{}$

$4 - 4 = \boxed{}$

$8 - 5 = \boxed{}$

$6 - 3 = \boxed{}$

$10 - 3 = \boxed{}$

$9 - 3 = \boxed{}$

$2 - 1 = \boxed{}$

$3 - 2 = \boxed{}$

$5 - 3 = \boxed{}$

$5 - 4 = \boxed{}$

$3 - 1 = \boxed{}$

$9 - 5 = \boxed{}$

$10 - 5 = \boxed{}$

$8 - 3 = \boxed{}$

$10 - 1 = \boxed{}$

$1 - 0 = \boxed{}$

$4 - 2 = \boxed{}$

$3 - 3 = \boxed{}$

$4 - 3 = \boxed{}$

$5 - 1 = \boxed{}$

$7 - 3 = \boxed{}$

$8 - 2 = \boxed{}$

$7 - 6 = \boxed{}$

$8 - 6 = \boxed{}$

Make Coin Collections

Name

Practice

Continue the pattern.

| R | R | E | E | R | R | E | E | | | | | | |

| △ | △ | △ | ◇ | △ | △ | △ | ◇ | | | | | | |

| 6 | 6 | 2 | 2 | 6 | 6 | 2 | 2 | | | | | | |

| △ | ○ | ▢ | △ | ○ | ▢ | | | | | | | | |

| O | S | S | O | S | S | | | | | | | | |

| ♡ | • | • | ♡ | • | • | ♡ | • | | | | | | |

| 7 | 4 | 2 | 7 | 4 | 2 | | | | | | | | |

| ☽ | ◇ | □ | ☽ | ◇ | □ | | | | | | | | |

| □ | □ | □ | ○ | □ | □ | □ | ○ | | | | | | |

| △ | △ | ▭ | △ | △ | ▭ | | | | | | | | |

🔄 **On the Back** Draw your own patterns.

Name _____

Introduction to Time

Name _____

Homework

Read the clock.

Write the time on the digital clock.

7:00

hour : minute

hour : minute

:

:

:

:

:

:

:

:

On the Back Draw a picture of a clock in your home.

Show and Write Times

Name _____

Homework

Ring the clock that shows the correct time.

Cross out the clock that shows the wrong time.

1.

11:00

2.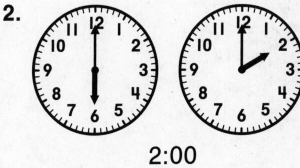

2:00

3.

5:00

4.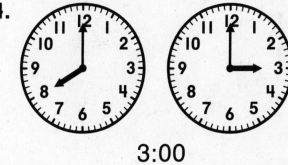

3:00

5.

10:00

6.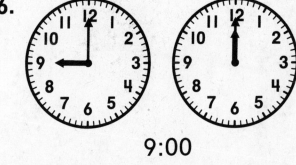

9:00

7.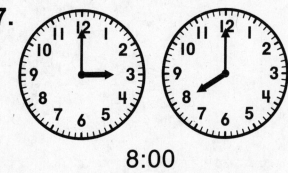

8:00

8.

1:00

 **On the Back** Draw a picture of what you do at 4:00 in the afternoon.

Time in Our World

Homework

Read the clock.

Write the time on the digital clock.

8:30

hour : minute

:

hour : minute

:

:

:

:

:

:

:

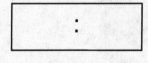

:

 On the Back Draw a digital clock. Write a time you know on it.

Time to the Half-Hour **181**

Time to the Half-Hour

Name _____

Homework

Use the calendar for questions 1 and 2.

			April			
Sunday	Monday	Tuesday	Wednesday	Thursday	Friday	Saturday
		1	2	3	4	5
6	7	8	9	10	11	12
13	14	15	16	17	18	19
20	21	22	23	24	25	26
27	28	29	30			

1. What month is it? _____

2. Put the days of the week in order from 1 to 7.

Tuesday Friday Thursday Monday Wednesday Saturday Sunday

___ ___ ___ ___ ___ ___ ___

3. About how long would a weather chart for 30 days take?

week   month

4. About how long would it take for a painting to dry?

day   month

➡ **On the Back** Choose a day, week, month, or year. Draw a picture of something that takes you that long.

Calendars **183**

Practice

Name _____

Find the totals.

Color each balloon as shown.

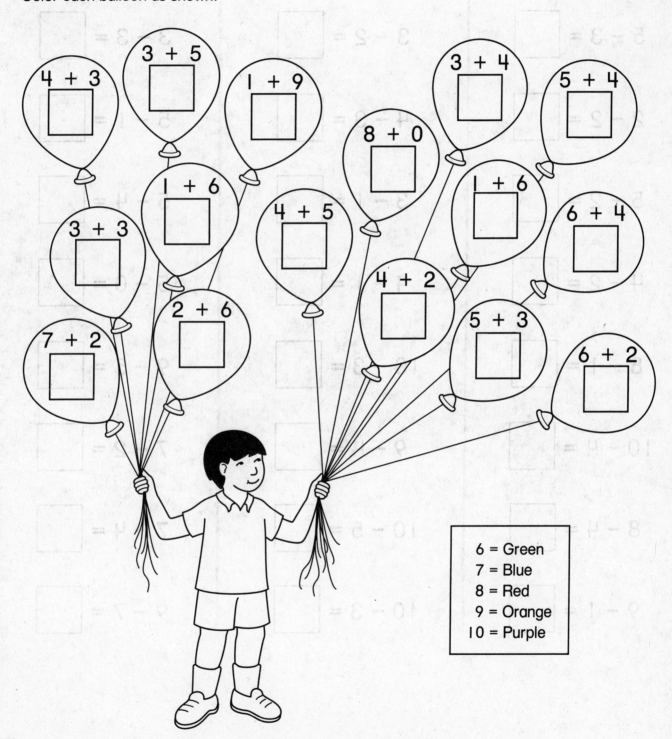

4 + 3	
3 + 5	
1 + 9	
3 + 4	
5 + 4	
8 + 0	
1 + 6	
3 + 3	
4 + 5	
1 + 6	
6 + 4	
2 + 6	
4 + 2	
7 + 2	
5 + 3	
6 + 2	

6 = Green
7 = Blue
8 = Red
9 = Orange
10 = Purple

On the Back Subtract the numbers.

1 − 0 = ☐   2 − 1 = ☐   4 − 0 = ☐

5 − 3 = ☐   3 − 2 = ☐   3 − 3 = ☐

2 − 2 = ☐   4 − 3 = ☐   5 − 1 = ☐

5 − 2 = ☐   3 − 1 = ☐   5 − 4 = ☐

4 − 2 = ☐   4 − 1 = ☐   5 − 0 = ☐

8 − 1 = ☐   10 − 3 = ☐   9 − 5 = ☐

10 − 4 = ☐   9 − 4 = ☐   7 − 2 = ☐

8 − 4 = ☐   10 − 5 = ☐   7 − 4 = ☐

9 − 1 = ☐   10 − 3 = ☐   9 − 7 = ☐

Name _____

Practice

Cross out shapes to make the groups equal.

1.
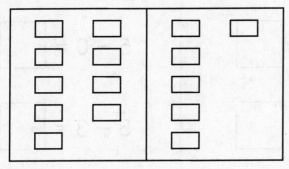

2.
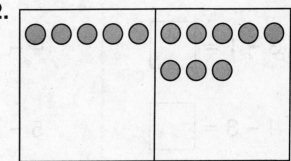

3.
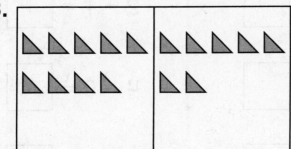

4.
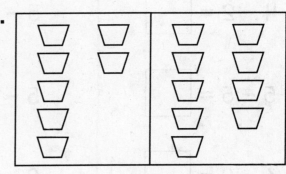

5.
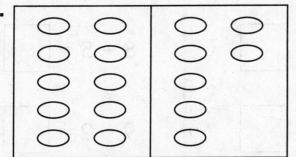

6.
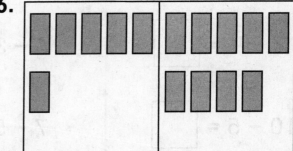

7.
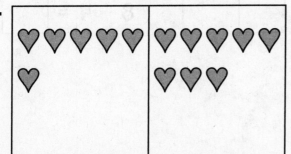

8.
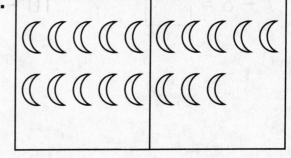

➡ **On the Back** Subtract the numbers.

1 – 1 = ☐   3 – 2 = ☐   2 – 2 = ☐

3 – 1 = ☐   4 – 1 = ☐   5 – 0 = ☐

4 – 3 = ☐   5 – 2 = ☐   5 – 3 = ☐

4 – 2 = ☐   5 – 4 = ☐   2 – 1 = ☐

5 – 5 = ☐   5 – 1 = ☐   4 – 0 = ☐

6 – 2 = ☐   8 – 3 = ☐   9 – 4 = ☐

7 – 4 = ☐   6 – 3 = ☐   8 – 5 = ☐

10 – 5 = ☐   7 – 5 = ☐   9 – 2 = ☐

7 – 6 = ☐   10 – 8 = ☐   8 – 4 = ☐

6-11

Name _____

Homework

1. Ring the object that is heavier. Underline the object that is lighter.

2. Order the objects from heaviest to lightest. Write the number.

_____   _____   _____

3. Ring the container that holds more. Underline the container that holds less.

4. Order the containers from the one that holds least the to the one that holds the most. Write the number.

_____   _____   _____

On the Back Draw 3 objects in order from lightest to heaviest.

Weight and Capacity

Name _____

Homework

1. Draw an item that is hot.

```



```

2. Draw an item that is cold.

```



```

Ring the item that is warmer. Underline the item that is cooler.

3.

4.

5.

⬤ **On the Back** Draw 2 outdoor scenes. Label them hot and cold.

Temperature

Homework

Write the numbers 1–120 in vertical columns.

10								2	1
									11
100									
120									

➡ **On the Back** Write the numbers 1–120 in horizontal rows.

1	2								10
11									
									100
									120

Numbers Through 120

Homework

Name _____

Read the number word.
Write the number in the box.
Color as shown.

6 = orange	9 = green
7 = yellow	10 = red
8 = purple	

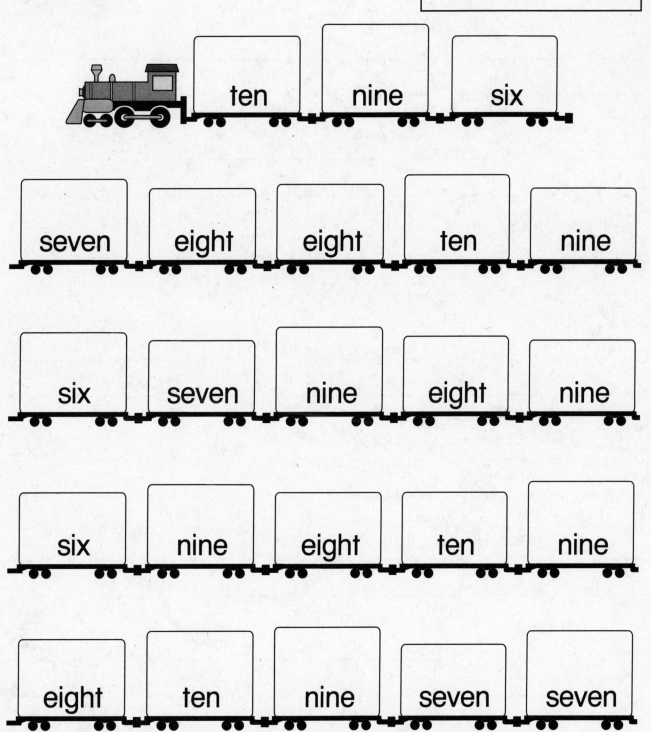

ten   nine   six

seven   eight   eight   ten   nine

six   seven   nine   eight   nine

six   nine   eight   ten   nine

eight   ten   nine   seven   seven

⬤ **On the Back** Write the number words for 1 through 10.

Name

Write Number Words

Name _____

Homework

Connect the dots in order.

1.

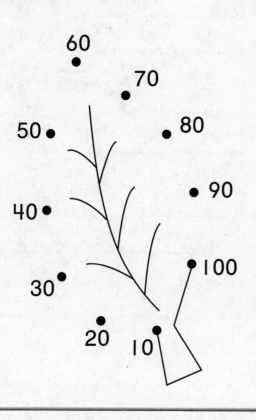

60
70
50
80
90
40
100
30
20
10

2.

40

45 50 30 35

5 25 20

10 15

Skip count.

3. 10, 20, 30, 40, _____, _____, _____, _____, _____, _____

4. 5, 10, 15, 20, _____, _____, _____, _____, _____, _____

5. 2, 4, 6, 8, _____, _____, _____, _____, _____, _____

➡ **On the Back** Continue counting by 2s starting with 20 ending with 50.

Counting Different Ways **197**

Counting Different Ways

Name _____

Homework

Use the data in the picture graphs to answer questions.

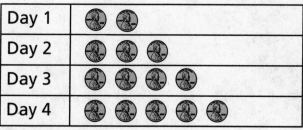

Pennies in Jar 1

Day 1	🪙 🪙 🪙 🪙 🪙
Day 2	🪙 🪙 🪙 🪙
Day 3	🪙 🪙 🪙
Day 4	🪙 🪙

🪙 **Means 1 penny**

Pennies in Jar 2

Day 1	🪙 🪙
Day 2	🪙 🪙 🪙
Day 3	🪙 🪙 🪙 🪙
Day 4	🪙 🪙 🪙 🪙 🪙

🪙 **Means 1 penny**

1. Write the day that has the most pennies in the Jar.

Jar 1 _____ Jar 2 _____

2. Write the day that has the least pennies in the Jar.

Jar 1 _____ Jar 2? _____

3. What pattern is happening in Jar 1 each day?

_____

4. What pattern is happening in Jar 2 each day?

_____

➤ **On the Back** On the top write Jar 1 Day 5 and draw how many pennies you think there will be. On the bottom write Jar 2 Day 5 and draw how many pennies you think there will be.

Homework

Ring fair or unfair.

1. Spin an A.

fair   unfair

2. Spin an A.

fair   unfair

Ring likely, unlikely, or certain.

3. Spin a banana.

likely   unlikely   certain

4. Spin an apple.

likely   unlikely   certain

5. Spin a piece of fruit.

likely   unlikely   certain

 On the Back Draw a spinner that is fair to spin a 1.